I0794909

IMAGES
of America

PARK CITY

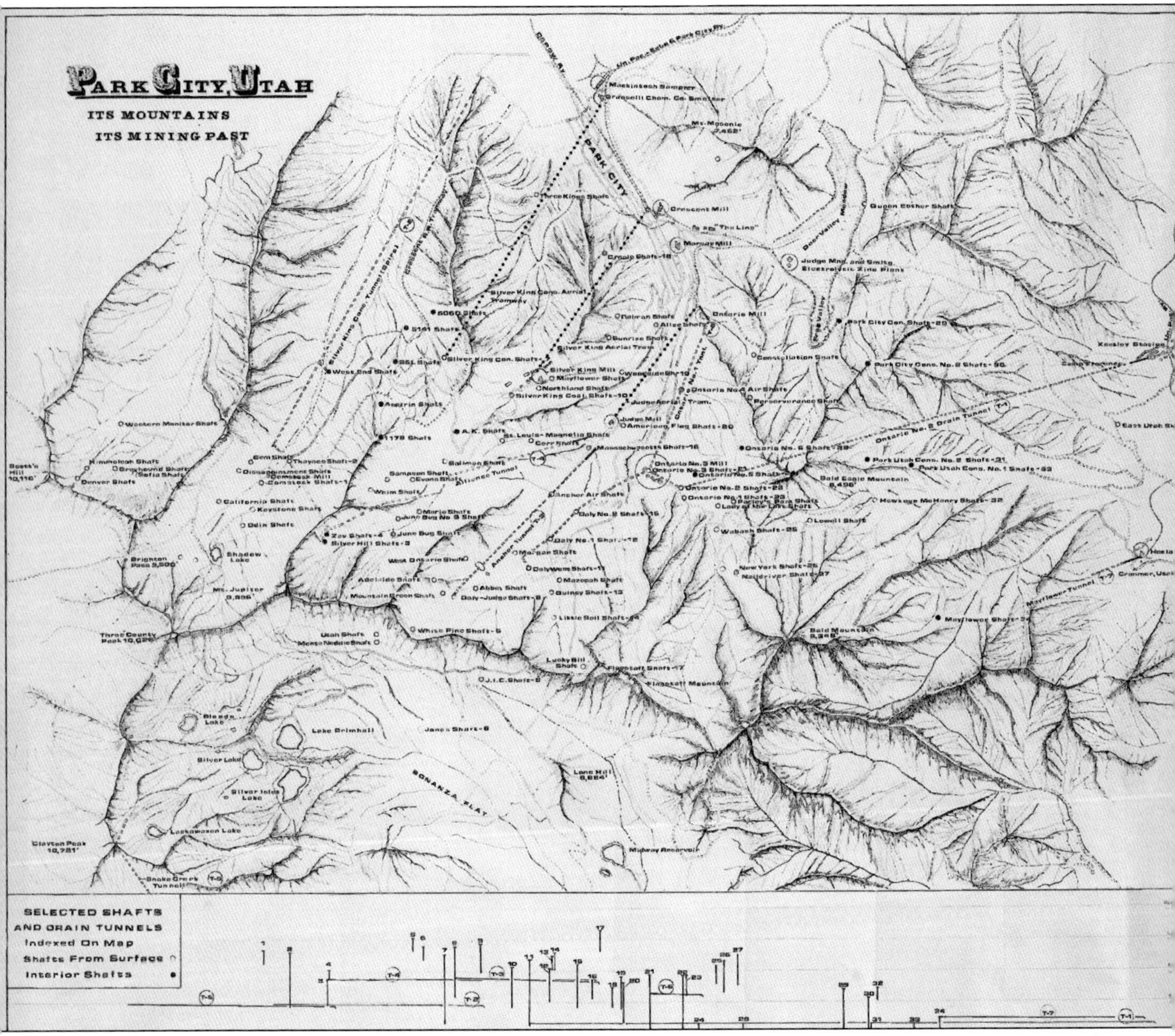

This map shows the location of many of Park City's most prominent mine shafts and drain tunnels. It contains a map to show locations along with a cross-section of how the shafts compare; in other words, how deep they were driven. (Courtesy of the Park City Historical Society & Museum.)

On the Cover: Two miners stand in an unidentified mine, holding shovels and sticking tommy candle holders, around the 1870s–1890s. (Courtesy of the Park City Historical Society & Museum.)

IMAGES
of America

PARK CITY

Dalton Gackle

ARCADIA
PUBLISHING

ISBN 978-1-4671-0842-3

Published by Arcadia Publishing
Charleston, South Carolina

Printed in the United States of America

Library of Congress Control Number: 2022931670

For all general information, please contact Arcadia Publishing:
Telephone 843-853-2070
Fax 843-853-0044
E-mail sales@arcadiapublishing.com
For customer service and orders:
Toll-Free 1-888-313-2665

Visit us on the Internet at www.arcadiapublishing.com

This book is dedicated to my grandparents, who all helped to nurture my love for history and writing.

Contents

Acknowledgments		6
Introduction		7
1.	Snyderville and Parley's Park City	9
2.	Discovery of Ore	17
3.	Early Park City	27
4.	The Great Fire of 1898	41
5.	Mines of Treasure Hill	53
6.	Mines of Ontario Canyon, Empire Canyon, and Beyond	79
7.	General Life in Park City	103
8.	Depression and Reevaluation of Economy	123
Index		127

ACKNOWLEDGMENTS

Thank you to the Park City Museum for letting me take on this project. Thank you to my co-workers, who supported the project. Thank you to Sally Elliott, who helped guide the direction of the book and shared her knowledge, expertise, and passion. Thank you to all who have contributed to Park City's incredible history.

Author proceeds from this book will go to the Park City Museum and its preservation group, the Friends of Ski Mountain Mining History, which is taking on the tireless work of preserving Park City's historic mining structures, many of which are at risk of collapse or total loss. More information and a donation page can be found at parkcityhistory.org.

All images used in this book come from the Park City Historical Society & Museum. Several images are further noted as having come from the museum's Pop Jenks Collection.

INTRODUCTION

This book covers Park City's history from its early settlement through the mid-20th century, when the town began a shift away from its foundation of mining. While a good amount of history is covered here, it is by no means comprehensive.

Settled by white Europeans in the early 1870s on the ancestral homes of several different tribes and bands of Native peoples, including the Ute, Goshute, Shoshone-Bannock, and Eastern Shoshone, Park City, Utah, sits in a high valley rich in natural resources.

Early settlement at the mouth of the Snyderville Basin and the development of the transcontinental railroad opened the door for exploitation of the area's mineral wealth. But while Native peoples had been in the area for centuries and white settlers had arrived by the 1850s, it was not until 1868 when a few men came across an outcropping of silver that would put Park City on its course.

Silver was first prospected by Ephraim Hanks and Rufus Walker on Treasure Hill, but Bonanza Flat near Bald Mountain is where the story takes off. The mining rights claimed there would become Park City's first ore-producing mine—the Flagstaff Mine. Once silver, lead, and zinc were leaving this first mine and other early mines, Park City's community grew into a bustling boomtown predicated on exporting silver ore. It did not take long for a massive mine to strike it big in Park City's plentiful, mineral-rich mountains. The Ontario Mine exploded and became one of the richest silver mines in the world's history.

Soon after, the Silver King Mining Company bought up several moderately successful claims grouped close together. As the company pushed deeper into the hills, it too found a bounty of silver and became one of the world's great silver producers.

Meanwhile, Park City was incorporated in 1884 while its population had continued to grow. Main Street expanded to see dozens of businesses arrive to serve the community. The *Park Record* was formed in 1880 and is the oldest continuously published non-daily newspaper in the United States. Immigrants from Europe flooded in to work in the mines. Migrants from other states joined as well, and many opened stores and other businesses to serve the community. Chinese immigrants who had worked on the Transcontinental Railroad and then a spur from Echo down to Park City settled in town, forming a small Chinatown on Swede Alley to the east of Main Street.

The town experienced a major setback in 1898 when a fire destroyed much of the town's core. Main Street almost entirely burnt down, along with Chinatown, most of Swede Alley, and parts of Park Avenue and other streets. Some in the state thought Park City was finished. But the town banded together and had fully rebuilt and even expanded within 18 months. Not only did the many people who had moved their lives to Park City not want to give up, but the lucrative silver hidden in the hills made sure almost everyone stayed.

Of course, mining was an incredibly difficult and dangerous profession. It still is, but labor regulations, safety improvements, and technology have improved the working conditions tremendously. Many miners lost their lives, either on the job from falls, explosions, or collapses (amongst other accidents) or because of the job, developing miners' consumption and other health issues. Park City's worst mining disaster occurred in 1902 after an explosion and subsequent release of noxious gasses in the Daly West and Ontario Mines.

The town continued to grow and saw several schools come and go, all near the heart of town. As a town of many immigrants, Park City also saw several denominations of Christian churches open their doors. Social halls and fraternal clubs sprang up around town, but the most popular gathering spots were the saloons; nearly every ethnicity in town had its own. At one point, Park City had over two dozen saloons, rare in a state where few other towns had one at all since Mormons are teetotalers.

Parkites built homes on the sides of the mountains on either side of Main Street, with each parallel street rising in elevation. More wealthy residents built their homes on Rossie Hill. Chinatown sat on Swede Alley, close to Main Street. Miners and others built shacks on Swede Alley, upper Main Street, Daly Avenue, and other small streets. More residents built small and medium Victorian homes along Park Avenue, Woodside Avenue, Norfolk Avenue, and other streets. Many of these homes remain today, along with the churches and two of the schools.

Park City's mining industry was always a steady producer, though the profits were not always steady. Financial panics and volatile metal prices fluctuated the income for mining companies. Park City faced many hard times but usually worked through them. But like the rest of the country, Park City experienced great hardship during the Great Depression, as metal prices plummeted. Prices improved with the advent of World War II but decreased again in the early 1950s and never recovered.

With mining on its way out, and with no clear signs of recovery, United Park City Mines, which by then controlled most of the mines in Park City, decided to try to make money in another way: on the surface of the mountains rather than underground. That is a story for another book.

Of course, that story of skiing in Park City is not without overlap with Park City's mining history. The development of skiing in Park City is tied to a mining company. And mining in Park City continued and struggled until 1982, when skiing took over for good. Despite the change in economic engine, Park City remembers its mining past. The remnants of mines still dot the hills along hiking trails and ski slopes. Some are even still utilized as the municipal government "mines" much of the town's water from the same tunnels that once birthed silver ore. Many of the town's mining-era buildings and homes still stand on Main Street and the rest of Old Town, after their own vacancy and near destruction. It is there, at the brink of Park City becoming a ghost town, where this book concludes, but not where Park City's history concludes.

One

Snyderville and Parley's Park City

From 1846 to 1847, Mormons, rejected from the Midwest, journeyed to the Utah Territory to make their new home. To reach the Salt Lake Valley, the travelers had gone through Emigration Canyon. This route continued to be used for a time, but it was not an ideal pass to get through the Wasatch Mountains.

Parley Pratt, a high-ranking member of the church and close friend of Brigham Young, set out to find a better way through the mountains. He ultimately surveyed and denoted a route through the Wasatch Range that is known as Parley's Canyon. The peak of the route is called Parley's Summit, and the Snyderville Basin, which holds Park City, lies just beyond that summit.

There, the Mormons set up a toll for travelers arriving at Salt Lake or heading on to California. Nearby, William Henry Kimball, a former general in the Mormon militia, established a stagecoach line and hotel in 1854 in what is now Kimball Junction. Moving inward through the basin sat a small community called Snyderville. It was named for early Mormon settler Samuel Comstock Snyder, who set up a sawmill in the 1850s to meet a demand for lumber in the area and around Salt Lake City.

The Snyderville Basin sits at a cross point of the ancestral homes of several different tribes and bands of Native peoples, including the Ute, Goshute, Shoshone-Bannock, and Eastern Shoshone. These people spent the warmer months hunting, fishing, gathering, camping, and living in the area. As the Mormons moved in, there was conflict, and Native peoples began to avoid the area.

The main work in Snyderville was farming and milling. Samuel Snyder came to settle the area after purchasing settlers' rights in 1848 from Parley P. Pratt. He was lured by the standing timber and immediately began to establish a sawmill (pictured) and farms. Both enterprises were enhanced by the discovery of ore in Park City. The farms fed the burgeoning mining population and the timber shored up the mining excavations. Early photographer A.J. Russell took this photograph around 1868 to 1869 during his time documenting the construction of the Union Pacific portion of the Transcontinental Railroad.

In this image, the Snyder home and farm are bustling with work. Stacks of timber sit around the property from the mill. The stable behind the home is full of horses being tended by farmhands. Other livestock congregate between the home and the stable. This image was also captured by A.J. Russell during the construction of the Union Pacific portion of the Transcontinental Railroad.

William H. Kimball built a large 11-room native stone hotel in the early 1860s for about $10,000 and served as postmaster, with his second plural wife, Melissa Burton Coray Kimball, performing the postal duties. This complex also served as the base for the Kimball Stage Station between Wyoming, Park City, and Salt Lake City. Noted guests of the hotel included Walt Whitman, Mark Twain, and Horace Greeley. The Transcontinental Railroad put the hotel out of business in 1869, but it was soon brought back with Park City's mining boom. The hotel is pictured above with coaches out front in 1872. Kimball eventually transformed the hotel into a ranch, pictured below with sheep herding along the road. The buildings are still visible north of Interstate 80 in Kimball Junction and are currently owned by the Bitner family.

Transportation and agriculture were critical industries in the early mining days of Park City. This photograph of the Kimball Stage Station, Hotel, and Ranch details the large number of buildings supporting both industries. The Kimball stage and hotel were part of the Overland Stage Route.

As a small but growing community, Snyderville needed a place to bury its dead. The Snyderville Cemetery is seen here in May 2000. It is now surrounded by a housing development, but remains intact.

Near present-day Lucky John Drive and Monitor Drive, the LDS Church owned a large farm to produce food for its worldwide system of Bishop's Storehouses to respond to emergencies and feed the hungry. It was also a way to provide employment for those temporarily out of work. The 840-acre farm seen here was sold for development to the Treasure Mountain Resort Company in 1971.

The Snyderville Basin and land surrounding Park City were home to six to eight large dairies in the early days. This photograph is of the Stoven Ranch, also known as the Spring Creek Angus Ranch, acquired by Leland Swaner in 1959. At his death, the family donated land in his honor, and other parcels were added as density rights transfers to create Swaner Nature Preserve, which is on a 190-acre remnant of the pictured ranch.

One of Park City's most recognizable landmarks is the big white barn that travelers see on their way into town, just after leaving Snyderville and entering Park City limits. The farm that sits on the west side of the road was first homesteaded by the Harrison McLane family in 1886. The McPolin family acquired the farm in 1896 and had added the iconic white barn by 1922. Later, Dr. D.A. Osguthorpe transformed the farm and barn into a successful dairy operation. By 1990, the Utah Department of Transportation needed additional land to widen Highway 224, which ran alongside the farm. The Osguthorpes agreed to sell about 200 acres with very old water rights to Park City Municipal for $4.4 million. In 1990, Highway 224 was widened, and the remaining land, including the barn, was preserved as open space.

Rhoda Snyder was the fifth plural wife of George Gideon Snyder, Mormon bishop of Wanship, gristmill owner, and Summit County's probate judge—and the first woman to establish a home in the district. She and George, pictured here, moved closer to where the mining camps were building a community.

George Snyder established his other wives and children on ranches nearby. Pictured are his 15 children from five wives. From left to right are (first row) Bismark Snyder, Lillie Snyder Evans, Zina Snyder, Creighton Snyder, Rilla Snyder, Gideon Snyder, Nellie Snyder Thiriot, and Ruby Snyder Brown; (second row) Horace Snyder, Wilson Isaac Snyder, Frank Snyder, Brigham Snyder, Willard Snyder, Louis Snyder, Louisa Snyder Alexander, Jennie Snyder, and Grant Snyder.

Pictured is George Snyder around 1880. He and Rhoda moved in 1872 to the corner of what is now Park Avenue and Heber Avenue and constructed a boardinghouse where Rhoda cooked for and served miners. Her boardinghouse was the first to accommodate miners. They also built Dexter Stables across the street and a sawmill up the hill just south of the intersection of King Road, Park Avenue, and Main Street. George Snyder is credited with naming the mining camp Parley's Park City on July 4, 1872, with a little flag made of torn bedsheets. He declared the area "pretty as a park."

Two

Discovery of Ore

While Native Americans had camped in, utilized, and roamed the area for centuries, and while Mormon settlers traversed the land, setting up farms, mills, and a stage line nearby, the hills around what is now Park City were untapped of their metals.

That changed in the second half of the 19th century, beginning with the advent of the Civil War. While Utah was still a territory and not involved in the South's fight to retain slavery, the Mormons—Brigham Young most prominently—sympathized with the South. To make sure the Union would not lose a vital corridor to California, Abraham Lincoln sent troops to Utah to keep an eye on the Mormons and to protect Union telegraph lines to the west coast. They established Fort Douglas at the base of the Wasatch Mountains, overlooking and sitting just east of Salt Lake City. The fort and troops stayed after the end of the war.

The troops stationed there had come from California after experiencing its Gold Rush. As such, commanding officer Col. Patrick Connor encouraged his men to prospect the Wasatch Range in their downtime. In 1868, soldiers crossed through Big Cottonwood Canyon and crested over the top of the range where they found an outcropping of silver. A storm approached, so they marked the area with a stick and a bandana or other piece of cloth, like a flag. This claim would become known as the Flagstaff Mine.

Nearby was an area called Lake Flat, as a shallow lake sat in a high valley south of what would become Park City. Eventually, around 700 miners called Lake Flat home, working the Flagstaff, Lady of the Lake, Naildriver, New York, and McHenry Mines, among others. Mining was on in Park City.

Park City's first ore-producing mine was the Flagstaff Mine in the upper reaches of present-day Deer Valley, discovered in 1868 by men from Col. Patrick E. Connor's outfit at Fort Douglas who spent their downtime searching the Wasatch Mountains for ore. Connor and his men had come from Gold Rush–era California and hoped to bring a similar rush of gentiles to Utah to outnumber the Mormons, who most in the United States hated or distrusted. The prospectors marked the spot with a visible ore outcropping by driving a stake in the ground and tying a bandana or other fabric to the top, similar to a flag, hence Flagstaff Mine. Pictured at left is one of the mine's buildings, and below is the Flagstaff Mine and its structures.

There is considerable debate on what mining claim was filed first or discovered first, but the Flagstaff Mine was the first to produce any ore in the Park City area. By the early 1870s, the mild success of the Flagstaff had drawn many other prospectors to the area who began exploring other hillsides. As the number of mining claims grew, so too did the town. Pictured is the Flagstaff Mine dump.

Pictured is the portal to the Flagstaff Mine. The mine was located in an area west of Lake Flat, a large but shallow lake surrounded by thousands of pine, spruce, and aspen trees.

Over by Lake Flat, the Lady of the Lake, Nail Driver, the New York, McHenry, and other mines opened. Lake Flat grew to be a small community with approximately 700 residents. Living conditions were tough, dealing with the harsh, unforgiving winters of cold and snow at over 8,000 feet of elevation. As well, the main road, McHenry Road, was a steep and dangerous wagon path. The discovery of more significant ore deposits of the Ontario, Judge, and Daly West Mines below Lake Flat in Park City's other hills slowed the development of the Lake Flat mines and its community. By the late 1890s, all mines and homes were abandoned. The lake left, too, unintentionally drained by the Ontario No. 2 drain tunnel, which was completed in 1894.

Pictured is the Wabash Mine, one of the early Lake Flat mines, viewed from the west. It was a little farther north than some of the others, not far from where the Ontario Mine would eventually dig some of its shafts. Lake Flat sat to the northeast of the view in this picture.

Another early Lake Flat Mine, the Lady of the Lake Mine, produced very little ore. The mine was claimed in 1868 but lasted only into the 1880s before it was abandoned. The remains of the shaft are pictured here.

Incorporated in 1869, beyond Lake Flat and beyond even the Flagstaff Mine, over in Bonanza Flat, was the Jones Bonanza Mine, also known as the J.I.C. Mine. Pictured here in 1902, this mine produced very little but was the most successful claim in the Bonanza Flat area.

After the Flagstaff Mine opened and produced ore, many other claims followed, though most never developed into full mines. One that did, just north of the Flagstaff, was the Quincy Mine in upper Empire Canyon. Incorporated in 1871, the Quincy was an early success for Park City until the Ontario, Daly Judge, and Daly West Mines nearby superseded it. Pictured are two ore wagons, each with a driver and a team of four horses facing right in front of a very large ore loading bin and ore chutes. It is supposedly from the Quincy Mine but is more likely the Ontario Mine.

Another of Park City's earlier mines was the (original) Mayflower Mine, not to be confused with a later Mayflower Mine that mostly extracted gold from its workings. The original Mayflower sat in Woodside Gulch and saw early investment from future mining magnates John Judge, Windsor V. Rice, David Keith, and Thomas Kearns. The Mayflower struck a solid vein of silver ore, making good money for those men, who turned around and invested in a new company: the Silver King Mining Company. The Silver King took over the Mayflower and other nearby claims and became one of the largest producers of silver ore in the world. Pictured are men at the Mayflower, shifting ore from ore bins into wagons drawn by horses.

The mining industry is known for impacting the local environments it inhabits. Not only does this include the minerals extracted from the earth but, especially in the 19th century, vast amounts of timber were needed in the mines for supports in the tunnels, as well as fuel for steam-powered pumps and other equipment. This meant mineworkers were sometimes used as loggers or in mills, such as these men pictured in a milling operation outside the Mayflower Mine. As Park City mines grew (along with the town, which needed wood for new buildings), the Snyderville Basin was deforested at a rapid rate. It is rare for Park City to have a tree over 100 years old today.

Treasure Hill's earliest mine was the Woodside Mine, sitting in the lower portion of Woodside Gulch. Started in 1872–1873, the mine was an immediate success. This view looks up into Woodside Gulch from the Woodside Mine tunnel. On the right, a man is sitting on a pile of timbers that would be used as supports for the mine tunnel. Down the center, rail tracks curve into the distance. Two wood buildings are on the left.

The Woodside Mine was one of several successful claims in Woodside Gulch. In 1906, the Woodside, along with the Silver King, (original) Mayflower, Northland, and the Tenderfoot Mines in the gulch were bought by David Keith and Thomas Kearns as part of their mining venture, the Silver King Mining Company. This 1891 photograph shows miners at the Woodside Mine portal.

The earliest mine to bring Park City its silver fame was the Ontario Mine, incorporated in 1872. This mine set the pace for Park City's silver production, providing high-quality ore in enormous quantities. This mine will be featured heavily in chapter six.

Three

Early Park City

Once ore was discovered in the area, it was only a matter of time before a rush of people came in. Most were prospectors and miners looking to strike it rich. But a community filled out as well, centered around a steep Main Street in a valley just below the new mines. Park City was incorporated as a municipality in 1884, dropping the Parley's portion of the name so as not to remain connected to a Mormon disciple. While there were Mormons in town and a Latter-Day Saints ward, Park City was a secular place largely made up of non-Mormons, the only majority unaffiliated large community in Utah at the time.

Outside of Main Street with its businesses, the new residents built their homes. Miners with families built rough shacks on the hillsides while more wealthy residents built solid Victorian homes on Rossie Hill, Woodside Avenue, and Park Avenue. Both miners' shacks and more elegant homes remain preserved today.

Most miners were single men, however, and the laws of Utah dictated that these unmarried men should live in boardinghouses. Early on, the mining companies controlled these boardinghouses, charging miners room and board directly from their wages. But after the Pullman Strike disaster in South Side Chicago, national attention turned to labor issues, especially company towns.

Utah passed a law in 1901 that prohibited mining companies from requiring their employees to live in company housing. It was a proactive, prohibitive law to keep the mines open and avoid a labor disaster. It would keep Park City from operating under a monopoly or oligarchy and allowed for more private boardinghouses to open on and around Main Street.

One of Park City's saddest stories is of Pearl Snyder, Park City's first birth (born 1877), who died at just 18 months old in February 1879. It was snowing heavily, but her father, George, made a casket and hitched up his team. Mother Rhoda dressed Pearl in her finest tiny outfit, and they struck out in the snowstorm to take her body to Salt Lake City for a proper burial. When they reached Kimball Junction, however, they were forced to turn the horses around and head back to Park City. They saw a bare patch of ground then just north of Park City where George stopped to hack out a depression for the little casket. The plan was to take her to Salt Lake City in the spring for burial in a proper cemetery, but when the snow melted and the wildflowers bloomed, they decided to leave her in place. That spot, which belonged to George and Rhoda Snyder, soon became Park City Cemetery.

Like any other community with a growing population, children were present. Park City's first school, built in 1875, was the Ontario School in Ontario Canyon. It was a large one-room schoolhouse. Funded by the Ontario Mine, it was too far from the hub of the town and quickly became too small for Park City's growing population. It was soon replaced by other Park City schools.

Park City needed several schools to keep up with the growth. Pictured here are students outside Park City High School (then located in the Lincoln School). From left to right are (first row) Sam Raddon, Lorenzo Muirbrook, Bill Moulding, Bessie Dority, Claire Stevenson, Mae Williams, Pearl Lowe, Maude Hurley, Lily Lanyan, and Bill O'Keefe; (second row) Montague Allen, unidentified, Murray Davis, Anna Deason, Florence Carpenter, teacher ? Gallagher, Ella Snyder, Frieda Funk, Willard McClellan, George Quinn, Jerome Paxton, Stewart McPhee, and Clarence Blocher Supt; (third row) Minnie Kervin, Lillian Funk, Mamie Fernette, and Minnie Critchlow. Jerry Harrington and Harry Freeman are standing at right in the window.

This view of Park City is from around 1882–1884 above the Ontario Mill looking north. It clearly shows the valley that the Park City community sits in below the mines in its hills. It also illustrates how barren many of the hills are, as the mines cleared the trees to make timber for mine tunnels, and other Parkites needed wood to build homes and businesses.

Main Street runs relatively north to south in Park City. This image is looking south (uphill). Telephone lines run up and down both sides of the street, an important technological advancement for the bustling boomtown. Aside from the horse-drawn wagons and the dirt road, Park City's Main Street looks very similar today, thanks to key historic preservation of many of the buildings.

This image was taken on July 4, 1885, showing an early look at Park City's Main Street. Again looking south, R.E. Squires's carpentry workshop is on the right, a dentist is next door, and a second-hand store is next to that. Many of the businesses are using false fronts as a way to advertise. At that time, Park City had dirt roads and wooden boardwalk-style sidewalks. The road was paved soon after the arrival of automobiles, but the wooden walkways remained into the 1970s.

Park City was fortunate to have two railroads in town for hauling ore, coal, and passengers. The Union Pacific Railroad arrived first in 1880 with a spur connecting to the transcontinental railroad up in Echo. The Denver & Rio Grande Western's line was first built as the Utah Central in 1890 up Parley's Canyon to the west. This photograph is in Parley's Canyon prior to the Denver & Rio Grande Western's acquiring the Utah Central in 1898. It was built as a narrow-gauge line but converted to standard gauge. The line was abandoned in 1946, and the tracks were pulled, though many of the grades are still visible.

Pictured is the Union Pacific Depot, the endpoint of the spur that ran from Echo to Park City and allowed Park City to ship ore to be processed elsewhere. The depot was always busy with travelers and shipments, including mail. The tracks visible in the foreground run right up to the end of Main Street. The depot still stands today, though rehabilitated after a major fire nearly destroyed it.

Park City's second train depot served the Denver & Rio Grande Railroad. It was located north of the Union Pacific Depot and one street west on Park Avenue. This photograph of the train pulled up to the platform was taken in 1891. Several people stand on the platform and the conductor and an engineer or brakeman lean out of the cab of the engine, while another man services the engine in the foreground, and a horse-drawn carriage is pulled up to the platform.

As a community living among pollutive mines (notice the haze in the background), Park City needed access to clean water. Pictured is Park City's first reservoir, the first Park City waterworks. Looking north down Empire Canyon toward Daly Avenue, there are three connected ponds on the right holding clean water or water ready to be cleaned. Above, a man drives a team of horses back up the canyon toward one of the mines with an empty ore wagon ready to be filled. In the center sits a home or a building related to the waterworks. The Union Concentrator, or processing facility, embraces the left side of the canyon wall in the back left, while Park City is visible in the haze beyond. The Union Concentrator can be seen beyond the horizon of the water below.

W.D. Sutton, pictured here, owned a meat market in Park City and later moved to Salt Lake City, where he became an owner and manager of the Newhouse Hotel. He also served as state treasurer, Utah legislator, and Park City council member.

The E.D. Sutton & Co. butcher shop sat in the upper half of Main Street. It provided fresh meat for the town, specializing in beef and pork. Started by brothers Ephraim and William in the late 1890s, the business experienced a setback early on when its shop was destroyed in Park City's Great Fire of 1898. The business then set up shop in the unharmed Union Pacific Depot until it could move into a new location.

Small communities like Park City needed to have a variety of outlets for social life. These came in the forms of saloons, fraternal and sororal societies, theater performances, and a wide range of public events and parties. One common event around the turn of the 20th century was masquerade balls. This photograph shows the Grand Mask Ball in Park City, hosted by the Silver King Miners Association on January 12, 1900. One prominent feature of the room is a row of electric lights running down the center of the ceiling and smaller electric lights along the walls. Park City was one of the first towns in Utah to get electricity, in 1889.

Church functions were also an important part of life for many Parkites. Beyond just attending service or mass, many people attended dances, classes, and other events at their churches. This 1890s photograph shows a group of people in Park City Community Church as part of Park City Sunday School for Punctuality and Attendance.

This view from out front of Swede Hall looking southeast shows the upper part of Old Town Park City, including parts of upper Main Street, Daly Avenue, and King Road. The view is looking directly down Hillside Avenue. The path on the left accesses the homes along Hillside Avenue.

This view from a distance behind Swede Hall, looking northwest, shows how dominant the structure was in Old Town. The railing on the right is alongside Hillside Avenue. Swede Hall was a social gathering space for Swedish and Finnish immigrants who had made their way to Park City. They also opened up the hall for dances twice a week, a grand ball every Wednesday, and a social evening on Saturdays for the rest of the town. The hall was built in 1909 but was demolished in the mid-1940s after failing a safety inspection in 1945.

This parade is part of a celebration of Park City's miners that takes place every year, called Miners' Day. Today, it is celebrated on Labor Day, but before that federal holiday was implemented, Parkites celebrated earlier in the summer. This was one of only a few days miners were allowed off each year as a holiday. This parade travels down Main Street, heading north; the parade goes north to this day, as no one wants to walk uphill.

Pictured is the Miners' Union Hall. The Miners' Union was necessary to improve labor conditions in Park City's mines. Not only was it a place for miners to meet and discuss labor issues, but the union provided miners healthcare by funding the construction and operation of the Miners Hospital in Park City. The mines did not want to provide healthcare to the miners, lest they lose profit, and Salt Lake was too far of a trip in case of many illnesses or injuries.

The Miners Hospital was completed in 1904 and offered Parkites a proper facility to treat injuries, recover from illnesses, and give birth. To maintain the building, pay the employees, and fund supplies and an ambulance, miners paid $1 per month out of their paychecks to the union.

In 1870, John A. Nelson moved his family of six children and his wife, Eliza, to Park City, taking up a Civil War veterans' exemption covering much of the land that is now the base area of Park City Mountain Resort. He had served as a colonel in the 10th Regiment US Colored Infantry Troops in the war, and the land was a typical reward for such service. This barn was up against the hill, and the house was closer to what is now Empire Avenue. Above the barn was Nelson's Three Kings Mine, largely developed after his death in 1880.

The Nelson family continued to live on the farm for another generation. Pictured is part of their fabulous garden. Eliza Nelson donated one acre of their land when the miners' union was looking for a place to build the Miners Hospital. The hospital sat about where the Silver King Hotel at 1485 Empire Avenue is today.

This postcard shows the interior of the Grand Opera House, which was completed in 1897. The photograph is taken from a high vantage point and shows the box seats to the right of the stage and most of the stage itself. The stage has a backdrop with an ornate tower, a garden with trees, and some other buildings in the background. The opera house was considered one of Park City's most magnificent buildings upon its completion. Unfortunately, it was only held in that prestige for a few months before it was destroyed in Park City's biggest disaster.

Four

The Great Fire of 1898

By 1898, Park City was a thriving community. It had several mining camps, hosted many homes along the primary streets, and featured a bustling Main Street. The only problem was almost everything was made of wood.

Early in the morning on June 19, 1898, a fire started in the American Hotel near the top of Main Street's east side. There is no official record for what caused the fire—it could not be determined. Speculation offered two options: the fire could have started in the hotel's kitchen or perhaps someone knocked over an oil lamp in a room. Regardless of how, the fire quickly took over the wood-built hotel.

From there, the fire worked its way up and down the east side of Main Street as men shot off pistols and mine whistles pierced the air to awaken the town to the disaster. Business owners and tenants further down Main Street tried to save inventory and possessions by throwing them out into the road before the fire reached their buildings. Unfortunately, the mostly flammable goods created a bridge for the fire to cross from one side of Main Street to the other. The fire crept up to Park Avenue, parallel to Main Street to the west. Swede Alley, and Chinatown with it, parallel to Main Street on the east, could not escape the fire either. All told, the fire destroyed over $1 million worth of property in 1898 money.

Main Street runs relatively north to south in Park City. This image is looking south (uphill). Two columns of men in suits and hats march toward the camera. It appears they are wearing ribbons, meaning this is likely a Miners' Day parade. The Ontario Mill stacks spew smoke at the top of the street. The large building with the American flag on the right is Ascheim's Mercantile, built in 1881. This photograph was taken in 1897 or 1898, as the recently built Opera House is visible in the background at left. The First National Bank and Rogers' store are in the left foreground. None of the buildings pictured would survive the fire.

This photograph of Main Street looks north (downhill). It notes a "busy day in Park City" as people patronize different businesses in the scene. Most clearly visible on the left is Park City's then post office, which moved to the other side of the street later on. This photo was taken in 1898, just weeks before the great fire. Most of Park City's buildings were built with wood.

This incredible shot shows a view of the great fire taken from Hillside Avenue above upper Main Street to Park City's south. Two pillars of smoke rise in the air above a cluster of houses, and bright flames illuminate the early morning sky.

This image showcases men using hoses to put out a fire at the Park City Hotel on Main Street. The upper level is destroyed. Some men with a hose spray water into that upper section from the building's left corner. This photograph is undated and might be from a large 1912 fire that also affected the hotel. The hotel was destroyed by fire and rebuilt in both 1898 and 1912.

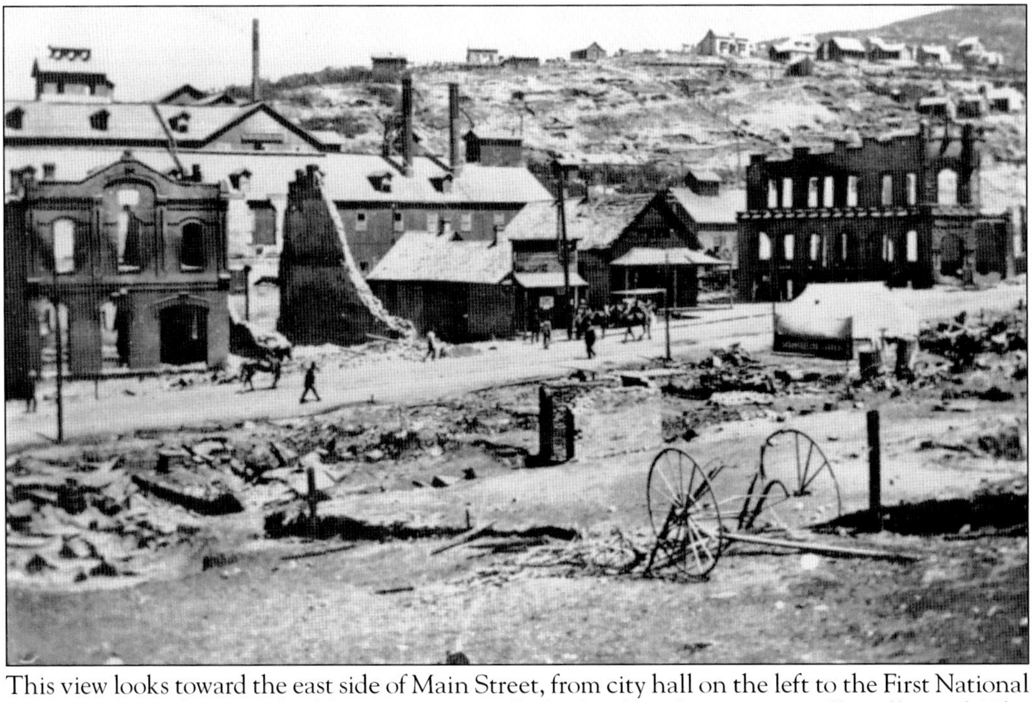

This view looks toward the east side of Main Street, from city hall on the left to the First National Bank on the right. Both buildings were partially built of brick, so some walls still stand. The Marsac Mill and a barren Rossie Hill sit in the background while the foreground shows Main Street's desolation. Only debris is visible except for one white tent and a fire hose wagon.

The *Park Record* newspaper office sat on Main Street in June 1898 before it was engulfed in flames. This tent took its place and the newspaper did not miss a single issue. Its June 29, 1898, edition chronicled the fire and detailed the damage done to the town. The headline across the top bemoaned "Park City's Awful Fire," while the subheadings gave readers a gut punch: "Over 200 business houses and dwellings destroyed. The loss over $1,000,000. Hundreds of people made homeless, many left destitute and scores of businessmen ruined—The heart of the city burned out—Very little insurance—Many firms will rebuild and commence anew."

This photograph captures the remains of city hall after the fire. The front facade at left is still largely intact while the south side is half destroyed. Originally built in 1885, the building was refurbished after the fire and served as Park City's city hall until 1983. The Park City Museum is partially housed in the building today, and the rafters in the original territorial jail on the lower level still bear the great fire's scorch marks.

This is all that remained of the Grand Opera House. Rossie Hill makes up the background, obscured by rubble still smoldering and releasing dark smoke. Two men and a boy pose in the brick rubble.

This photograph gives a good look at the expanse of the fire. Looking south up Main Street, rubble makes up the foreground. Houses that survived the fire on the west side of Park Avenue are on the right. Five men are walking up the center of the street. Smoke continues to rise from buildings up the street.

This photograph of Main Street features the remains of city hall and the First National Bank as people survey the damage. Viewed from the north, the visible outer walls of city hall remain intact, along with the corner of the bank up the street. Surprisingly, two wooden buildings remain standing and in apparently decent condition between the two brick structures that suffered heavy damage.

This photograph shows the same buildings from the opposite view, looking north down Main Street. The southern walls of the bank and city hall are destroyed, along with the entire interior of the bank. Many men and boys sit amongst the still-smoldering remains.

Rear of Grand Opera House,1898, Park City Utah

This postcard shows the remains of the Grand Opera House from its back side on Swede Alley. A group of men are using a firehose pump, drawing water from Poison Ditch (now Poison Creek) in the foreground. The air is clouded with smoke, but heavy damage to some small buildings is still visible in the background.

Remains of 1st National Bank,1898,Park City,Utah

This postcard shows the remains, or rather lack thereof, of the inside of the First National Bank. The bank vault in the back is still intact, though if any money or valuables survived inside is not known.

This postcard shows Crescent Corner after the fire. It offers an up-close look at the charred wooden boardwalk that ran alongside Main Street in front of businesses on either side. The remains of a building collapsed into its foundation are visible just beyond the walkway.

Almost immediately after the fire, Parkites began to rebuild. The *Park Record* set up a tent to publish the newspaper. In this image, George Wanning's Saloon is visible on the right, merely a shack amongst the rubble. His establishment was popular in a town of many saloons, and he made sure to continue serving Parkites despite losing his original building.

Temporary P O. After Fire

Park City, Utah

Park City began the slow process of cleaning up and rebuilding. Some businesses moved to buildings that were still standing, while others set up temporary structures while awaiting their new ones to be constructed. Pictured is the temporary post office after the great fire. A group of men and boys are gathered outside on the front porch of the building. The building itself has wooden siding and a metal awning.

The Dewey Theater, pictured here in November 1899, was erected after the fire. Not only did Park City rebuild almost all it had lost in just 18 months, but it expanded, including buildings like this theater. Many people line the walkway outside the theater. Sigvart Jensen stands by his barber pole.

Five

Mines of Treasure Hill

West and southwest of Park City, Treasure Hill provided miners with its namesake. Some of the most successful mines in Park City sat in the gulches throughout Treasure Hill. The Silver King, the Silver King Consolidated, California-Comstock, Keith-Kearns, Keystone, Northland, Woodside, and (old) Mayflower Mines made up many of the claims in the area. The Silver King Mining Company took over several of these mines, including the Silver King and Mayflower, to become one of the most successful mining companies in the world.

The Silver King continued to take over Treasure Hill, buying up other mines like the Silver King Consolidated, and becoming the Silver King Coalition Mines Company. In 1917, it bought a nearly completed drain tunnel from Solon Spiro, who was hoping the tunnel would finance itself with valuable ore found along its route. He had little luck in that regard and sold to the coalition. After digging just a few more feet, the mining company struck an incredibly rich vein.

The Silver King Coalition was a large production, and shipping ore down the mountain proved to be tedious. First mules and then the Crescent Tram narrow-gauge rail line brought ore down to where the Union Pacific came into town, but at a slow pace, especially in the winter. To expedite sending ore down the mountain, they installed an aerial tramway from the mill at the top down to a loading station, where Denver & Rio Grande railcars could pull straight in to be loaded. United Park City Mines Company took over the coalition and most of the rest of Park City's mines in 1953.

Treasure Hill is the main mountainside that overlooks Park City from the west. Pictured here in the background behind Park City around the 1910s, Treasure Hill lived up to its name, producing a large amount of silver ore. Treasure Hill is now protected open space, and several ski runs at

Park City Mountain Resort cut through its slope. This photograph gives another good look at hills devoid of trees after they were cut down to serve the town and the mines.

One of Treasure Hill's earliest mines was this, the Crescent Mine. Originally called the Pinyon Mine, it was on the east side of Thaynes Canyon. The Crescent Mine buildings and mine portal (to the right of the buildings) are all visible here, as is a large waste rock dump downhill to the left. The mine operated from 1882 until 1902.

The Crescent Mine needed a way to get its ore from the mine down to the railroad in town. In 1883, the Crescent Mining Company, run by E.P. Ferry, constructed a surface boardwalk tramway. It was initially utilized by mule teams hauling ore cars, but rail tracks were added in 1885, and a Shea engine was purchased to run the rail. The operation was smooth in the summer, though fairly slow with a steep grade and many curves along the way. In the winter, snow often piled up, blocking the tracks until they could be cleared, sometimes not for several days. When the Silver King Mining Company absorbed the Crescent Mine, it took over the Crescent Tram as well.

These were the four original mines of Woodside Gulch, all of which saw some degree of success. They were all acquired in 1892 by David Keith, Thomas Kearns, and others, along with several other mines, as part of the Silver King Mining Company. Another round of acquisitions a few years later made them part of the Silver King Coalition Mines Company.

Pictured is the base of Woodside Gulch at the edge of Old Town. King Road, which leads to the Silver King Mine, snakes past a home and up into the gulch.

This view of Park City gives a good look at Woodside Gulch. Empire Canyon rises from town at the left. Just left of center extending into the dark trees is Woodside Gulch. King Road begins at the point where the gulch and the homes meet and travels to the right at an upward angle, then zigzags back and forth as it heads toward the Silver King Mine further up the gulch.

The Silver King Mine in Woodside Gulch was formed in 1885 and had immediate and lucrative success. David Keith and Thomas Kearns took over the mine's lease. The massive profits from the Silver King allowed them to acquire other mines nearby and incorporate the Silver King Mining Company in 1892. The mine is pictured here in 1891 before that merger and the mine's expansion.

Pictured is the (original) Mayflower Mine in Woodside Gulch in 1891. While it had been claimed in 1880, the property was not worked until 1888. The lessees working on the mine needed capital, so they were joined by David Keith and Thomas Kearns in 1889. After the mine struck big soon after, Kearns and Keith, along with a few trusted friends, set out to prospect around the rest of Treasure Hill. After finding high-grade ore near the Mayflower, the prospecting party allegedly agreed to keep quiet while Keith and Kearns went about securing leases on as many of the claims on Treasure Hill as they could to form the Silver King Mining Company.

Albion Emery moved to Park City in 1880. He became the town's postmaster and was later elected speaker of the house in Utah's territorial legislature and grand master of the Utah Masonic Order. In 1884, he met and married Susanna Bransford, later known as Park City's Silver Queen. Albion switched gears to work in the Daly Mine, where he could earn a bit more money. Daly Mine superintendent David Keith and investor Thomas Kearns offered the Emerys an investment opportunity in the Mayflower Mine. Albion accepted and borrowed $8,000 from mining magnate R.C. Chambers, who he repaid in little time as the Mayflower struck it big. The Emerys then bought almost 25,000 shares of the newly incorporated Silver King Mining Company in 1892. That mine gave them enormous riches, allowing them to move to a Salt Lake mansion and become socialites. Albion passed away in 1894.

Pictured is the Northland Mine in Woodside Gulch. It was formed in 1888 and saw early success. That success, along with its proximity to the Silver King Mine, helped it to become one of the founding mines of the Silver King Mining Company.

Ezra Thompson was director of the Northland Mine before joining the Silver King Mine as its director for a short time. Thompson was born in Salt Lake City in 1850 and later moved up to Park City to work in the burgeoning mining industry. He served two terms on the city council in Park City before becoming mayor of Salt Lake City. He served as the 12th and 14th mayor of Salt Lake City, first for the Republican Party and then for the anti-Mormon American Party. He served two terms in his first stint and one term in his second, resigning due to ill health and a scandal in his administration.

Pictured are David Keith (left) and Thomas Kearns in an unknown mine. These two men invested in several of the mines in Woodside Gulch before forming the Silver King Mining Company in 1892 with the Silver King, Mayflower, Northland, and Woodside Mines. The Silver King Mining Company became one of the most successful mining companies in the world and gave both men enormous wealth. Their partnership went beyond mining; after moving to mansions in Salt Lake City, the men bought the *Salt Lake Tribune* and influenced it to become a prominent anti-Mormon voice in Utah. Thomas Kearns later served as a US senator from Utah. His wife donated their mansion to the state in 1937 to be used as the Utah Governor's Mansion; it still serves as such today.

Pictured is the Silver King Mine and Mill complex in Woodside Gulch in 1901, looking uphill due west. At the left of the image is the sampler building (erected in 1901) with a smokestack on its left. On the right is the large mill building extending down the hillside, with many dormers on its roof. This mill burned down in 1922. An inclined conveyor leads from the bottom of the mill up to the sampler. A covered tramway transporting ore from the mine extends behind the sampler to the top of the mill. An aerial tramway extends along the ridge of the hillside above the mill building. Up the hillside are two wooden water tanks (now called the Silver Queen tanks). The hoisting works and shaft buildings, along with the Silver King Boarding House and offices, are out of view to the left.

This 1905 postcard offers a slightly fuller picture of the Silver King Mine and Mill complex. This time, the shaft buildings are just visible at left. Two years later, the Silver King Mining Company acquired another group of mines, most prominently all the holdings of the Silver King Consolidated Mining Company in Thaynes Canyon. With those new mines, the company was renamed the Silver King Coalition Mines Company.

The closest mine to town was the Creole Mine on Treasure Hill. Located just above Old Town around Eighth Street, the claims that made up this mine were first patented between 1880 and 1882. By 1892, there were two shafts at the mine, joined shortly by a third. The mine was bought by more experienced miners in 1902 and was acquired by the Uintah Treasure Hill Mines Company in 1907. That company was absorbed by the Silver King Coalition Mines Company in 1910.

The Silver King Mine and Mill complex is pictured here around 1910 after its namesake company became Silver King Coalition Mines Company, this time from the east. The boardinghouse and offices sit in the lower left, while the shaft and hoisting buildings are at lower right. In the upper left, the sampler and some of the mill are visible. In the background are the water tanks and the waste rock dump, angled down the hillside at the specific angle of repose where loose material is stable.

Pictured is an up-close view of the Silver King Boarding House and offices. Miners slept and ate at this building, and the mine management took care of logistics, payroll, and other duties here. (Courtesy of the Pop Jenks Collection, Park City Historical Society & Museum.)

Pictured are the remains of the Silver King Mine's mill after a fire in 1921. An important operation of the mine, it was quickly rebuilt. The new mill was opened in 1922.

This image shows the Silver King Mine and Mill complex once again, this time in 1925 with the rebuilt mill. The new mill had a sloped roof and a more streamlined look as opposed to the original mill, which featured many dormers in the roof.

This image shows the Silver King Mine complex again from the west, this time with the newly rebuilt mill hidden from view. In the upper left are three smokestacks where the power plant, hoisting works, and shaft buildings are located. The white building in the back center is the Silver King Boarding House and offices. In the center is the sampler building. Out of view to the right is the mill building. An inclined conveyor leads from the bottom of the out-of-view mill up to the sampler. A covered tramway transporting ore from the mine extends behind the sampler leading to the top of the out-of-view mill. At the top of the image high up the hillside are the two wooden water tanks. A large waste rock dump sits at left. (Courtesy of the Pop Jenks Collection, Park City Historical Society & Museum.)

The Silver King Mine was a very successful mine that produced a high volume of high-quality silver ore. By the time the 19th century was coming to a close, sending ore down the mountain by mule or horse teams or through the Crescent tramway was too slow to keep up with the production at the mine and mill. The mine needed a new way to efficiently and quickly send ore down to town to be shipped out to Salt Lake City's smelters. Work on the Silver King Aerial Tramway began in August 1900. The construction was scheduled to be done in 90 days and employ 50 men and would cost over $17,000 in metal, cable, lumber, and labor. By the time it was finished, the tramway and its towers stretched over 7,000 feet from the Silver King Mine and Mill complex down to the newly constructed Silver King Coalition Building. The tramway system was fully operational by June 6, 1901.

Pictured is the Silver King Coalition building. Built in 1901 along with the Silver King Aerial Tramway, this building received ore buckets brought down from the Silver King Mine via the tramway and dumped into Denver & Rio Grande railroad cars for shipment to Salt Lake City and beyond. The enormous Coalition Building stood in Old Town at Park Avenue and Seventh Street until it burned in 1981. (Courtesy of the Pop Jenks Collection, Park City Historical Society & Museum.)

Three men seeking warmth after they could not return to Salt Lake City after a concert at Park City's Park West ski resort entered the Silver King Coalition building late at night on July 19, 1981. They started a fire on the floor of the building to keep warm. They thought they heard someone coming, so they extinguished the flames quickly and hid in a nearby abandoned railcar. They had not, in fact, put out the fire, and by the early morning of July 20, 1981, Park City's most iconic building was engulfed in flames.

Pictured is the Silver King Consolidated Mine, owned by Solon Spiro, in 1915. The view looks south and shows the boardinghouse at center; headframe, hoist building, powerhouse, and smokestacks at right; and covered tramway at left. The Silver King Consolidated Mine, not to be confused with the Silver King Mine, was a strong producer, but was nowhere near as successful as its rival Silver King. Likely as a way to tell it apart from the Silver King Mine, the Silver King Consolidated Mine was referred to as the "King Con."

The King Con Mine is pictured from the other side in this view. The mine's main claims centered on a shaft dug by John Bogan and his men in the 1880s. Bogan had patented several claims in Thaynes Canyon in 1880. He did not have the finances to extend his operation and was soon in debt to the Ascheim General Store. To settle his debt, he gave the store 5,000 shares of his mining company. The owner of the store, M.S. Ascheim, had a nephew named Solon Spiro who purchased the shares, thereby taking control of the Bogan Silver Mining Company and renaming it the Silver King Consolidated Mining Company. While it was a solid producer, declining silver prices after World War I made it difficult for the company to afford production costs. In 1924, the Silver King Consolidated Mining Company sold all of its workings and rights to the Silver King Coalition Mines Company for $600,000.

Miners stand in the elevator shaft at the King Con Mine. They wear yellow slickers to keep them dry and warm in the cool, wet tunnels of the mine. The cage, as the elevators were called, had a small roof on top to prevent falling rocks from hitting the men. However, it had no walls on two sides, so miners had to be careful to keep their limbs inside so as not to lose them. They also had to be sure to keep their balance so as not to fall out into the deep shaft.

Keeping a mine running smoothly required a lot of heavy machinery, whether it be for pumps, railcars, machine shops, or elevator equipment. This large piece of equipment is just one piece for the hoisting equipment that helped the elevators run up and down the shaft. This one was used in the Daly West Mine but is pictured on its way from there to the Silver King Consolidated Mine.

Above, a team of horses are hauling heavy machinery up to the Silver King Consolidated Mine. Below, men are trying to leverage what is likely a wheel for a water pump off of the bed it was hauled in on. Pumps were necessary for many mines in Park City, as the underground conditions are perfect for storing water from snowmelt and precipitation. These two photographs were taken in 1905.

The Silver King Consolidated Mine also had an aerial tramway with suspended ore buckets. It was built in 1916 to transport ore from the Silver King Consolidated Mine to the King Con Mill at the northern edge of Park City. The King Con tramway towers were built of wood.

The King Con aerial tramway terminated at the Silver King Consolidated Mill at Park City's north end. Pictured is the mill and the last tramway tower before the mill. This mill separated ore and waste rock and then, like the Silver King Coalition Building, dropped ore into railcars to be shipped to Salt Lake City's smelters.

Solon Spiro owned most of the claims in Thaynes Canyon through the Silver King Consolidated Mining Company. One that he did not own initially was the California Comstock Mine in upper Thaynes Canyon. The California-Comstock came to fruition after the separate California and Comstock Mines had legal troubles over ore mined from adjoining claims. They incorporated together in 1906 as the C&C Consolidated Mining Company. With his namesake tunnel heading straight for the California Comstock, Spiro and his Silver King Consolidated Mining Company bought the mine in 1918.

The Comstock Mine in upper Thaynes Canyon was a complete operation. It had the shaft and hoisting works, an office and boardinghouse, and a mill. Pictured is the mill before the California-Comstock Mine was acquired by the Silver King Consolidated Mining Company.

The California Comstock mill building is one of many mining structures still standing in Park City's mountains, now among the hiking trails and ski runs. It is pictured here in the 1990s. It has since been stabilized but needs much more preservation work, which is being undertaken by the Park City Museum's Friends of Ski Mountain Mining History preservation group.

Solon Spiro spent several years driving a 14,000-foot-long development and exploration tunnel to his mine claims in Thaynes Canyon beginning in 1916. The route surveyed was believed to contain valuable ore. By 1920, the tunnel extended to 12,500 feet but had extracted little ore. In April 1921, the tunnel had reached 14,250 feet but saw more water than anything else. By 1923, the King Con needed more financing for the project. Ultimately, Solon Spiro sold his King Con mine and namesake tunnel to the Silver King Coalition Mines Company in 1924, not having found anything of value after over 14,000 feet. The coalition dug only a few hundred more feet before it struck valuable ore. Pictured is the portal to the tunnel before its sale.

The Spiro Tunnel was plagued by heavy-flowing water the deeper it extended. Today, much of Park City's water supply comes from the mountains, flowing through mine drain tunnels on its way to the treatment plant, including through the old Spiro Tunnel.

The Silver King Coalition Mines Company built the Thaynes Shaft in the 1930s to connect the Spiro Tunnel with its other holdings beyond Thaynes Canyon. Although the shaft was no longer used for mining by the late 1950s, it, along with the Spiro Tunnel, was converted to a ski lift of sorts for the new Treasure Mountains Resort in 1965, and ran for just four years.

The Silver King Mining Company bought the Alliance Mining Company in 1899 and the Crescent Mining Company in 1903. It built crosscuts from its Silver King holdings to the Alliance, and after purchasing the Crescent holdings, added crosscuts and raises to reach the Crescent's Hanauer, Aetna, and Jones Tunnels, as well as the Apex Mine. After the 1903 purchase, Keith and Kearns built a mill near the portal of the Hanauer Tunnel to handle ore coming from their recently acquired holdings. They called this mill, pictured here, the Kearns-Keith Mill.

The Alliance Mining Company began driving the Alliance Tunnel in May 1889 and finished in August 1890. The tunnel extends from the mouth of Walker Webster Gulch in Empire Canyon 4,576 feet west into the gulch. It was originally driven to drain water from the old Sampson Mine workings up the gulch. The tunnel marks the crossover point from the Treasure Hill mines to the Empire Canyon Mines, or rather the crossover from the Silver King Coalition Mines Company holdings like the Silver King Mine to the Park Utah Consolidated Mines Company holdings like the Daly West and Ontario Mines. Although no actual mine existed for the company, some ore was found during the driving of the tunnel, which helped offset the tunnel cost. The Silver King Mining Company bought the Alliance Mining Company in 1899. Pictured is the Silver King Coalition Mines Company 1935 Alliance Tunnel crew.

Six

Mines of Ontario Canyon, Empire Canyon, and Beyond

One of Park City's most successful mines was claimed early: the Ontario Mine was claimed in 1872 after prospectors found especially rich silver ore. Mining mogul and later US senator George Hearst was looking to invest in Park City and had R.C. Chambers, a trusted associate, scouting for good claims. Chambers found the Ontario claim and convinced Hearst that this was the opportunity he was looking for. Hearst paid $27,000 for the claim—a large sum, but an investment where the gains far exceeded the initial cost.

The Ontario Mine sits in Ontario Canyon (with three shafts at different points along it), which is east of Empire Canyon and stretches from Park City's southeast end south toward Flagstaff Mountain. The Wabash and Naildriver Mines, among others, also sat in the upper reaches of this canyon.

Extending southwest from Park City's southern end, then curving back southeast is Empire Canyon. Toward the end of this canyon, several successful mines opened, including the Daly, the Daly West, the Daly Judge, the Massachusetts, the Quincy, and the Little Bell Mines. The tunnels of some of these mines reached those in Ontario Canyon to the east. It was in these tunnels that Park City's worst mining disaster occurred in 1902, affecting the Daly West and Ontario Mines. In 1925, these mines all fell under the ownership of one company, the Park Utah Consolidated Mines Company. That company joined the Silver King Coalition Mines Co. to become United Park City Mines Co. in 1953.

East of Flagstaff Mountain is Bald Mountain. Just south of its peak sat the Star of Utah and (new) Mayflower Mines. Eventually, the Mayflower was the last remaining mine being worked in Park City. East of there, the mining community of Keetley worked. One of Park City's unluckiest mines, the Park City Consolidated, sat east of Rossie Hill in the far reaches of Deer Valley.

This c. 1877–1884 view of upper Park City offers a good look at Ontario and Empire Canyons. Ontario Canyon starts at the top left and heads toward the top-right behind the ridge. Empire Canyon starts in the center of the image and heads toward the top-right corner. The Ontario Mill is visible at top left at the base of Ontario Canyon.

A group of investors from Michigan, called "the Michigan Bunch," looking to capitalize in Park City noticed that shipping ore to Echo or down to Salt Lake was inefficient and the ore full of waste. To solve the issue, they built the Marsac Mill, pictured before 1898, on the southeast edge of town. This facility would reduce mined ore down to its most valuable components by crushing it and separating out the waste rock. The mill operated between 20 and 30 crushing stamps that ran 24 hours each day. The mill processed ore from the Michigan Bunch's Flagstaff Mine and charged other mines a hefty sum to do the same. For a while, it and the McHenry Mill were the only mills in town. But by 1904, there were several other mills in Park City, including mills for the Ontario, Daly Judge, and Silver King Mines—the three producing the most. The Marsac Mill ceased production and was torn down.

Pictured is the main shaft of the Ontario Mine in 1881. The Ontario, formed in 1872, became one of the biggest producers of silver in the world. This is the mine that put Park City on the map in its early days, drawing attention from more miners and investors.

A mule is hooked up to a train of ore cars on a rail outside the Ontario No. 1 Tunnel. The ore cars hold at least nine miners. All miners as well as the mule are wearing slickers to keep them dry and warm in the cool, wet conditions inside the mine. Mules were trained to pull a certain number of cars and often would refuse to pull a train if there were more cars than usual; they could hear how many cars were hitched together behind them.

Four men stand facing the camera at the 1,500-foot level of the Ontario Mine. R.C. Chambers, who encouraged George Hearst to buy the rights to the Ontario claim and the mine's superintendent, leans against the mine car holding a lantern. The elevator cage is in the background while multiple loaded ore cars are at right.

R.C. Chambers is seated at a desk in the Ontario Silver Mining Co. office. The calendar on the wall reads January 1900. Hearst had offered Chambers one-third of the interests in any mine that Chambers acquired for him. If Chambers never invested in any other mines, he still would have been a millionaire due to the success of the Ontario.

This is the Ontario Mine boardinghouse in 1891. Single miners were required by Utah law to live in a boardinghouse at this time. There were a couple of independent boardinghouses in town by 1891, but most miners lived in company housing. The Ontario Mine took rent for room and board directly out of miners' paychecks.

At $100 per ton, the ore near the Ontario's surface was valuable, but deeper ore could consistently bring $150 per ton. However, the deeper the mine went, the more water flooded in. In 1881, owner George Hearst commissioned Cornish workmen in Philadelphia to construct a huge pump to take water out of the mine. The pump was modeled after steam engines used to remove water from the mines of Cornwall, England, so it was named the "Cornish Pump." While it was being put together, miners constructed Ontario Mine Shaft No. 3 to house it. The pump's parts were transported to Park City and reassembled. The enormous flywheel measured 30 feet in diameter and weighed 70 tons. The pump's construction and installation cost $250,000, but due to the Ontario's success, it more than paid for itself, pumping water from the 1,000-foot level up and out of the Ontario No. 1 drain tunnel at the 600-foot-level. The pump was rendered useless after the gravity-driven Ontario Drain Tunnel No. 2, which went out to Keetley and could drain water from the No. 3 shaft's 1,500-foot level, opened in 1890. The image at right is from 1891.

Legend has it that one day in the mid-1880s, the pump froze. A mechanic was called to get it running, as the men could not mine without it pumping water out. The mechanic looked over the pump, climbed up the flywheel, took a sledgehammer, and swung down a single blow, springing the pump back to life. The mechanic billed the mine $100 for his work—a hefty sum for such a simple act. Incensed, they demanded an itemized bill for his services. The mechanic replied, "For hitting the flywheel with the hammer, 50¢; for knowing where to hit it, $99.50."

All three Ontario Mine shafts are visible in this image looking down Ontario Canyon. Massive waste rock dumps are seen toward the top, settled at the angle of repose. The boardinghouse sits at bottom right with the other mine buildings spread throughout.

Pictured is an early Ontario Mine crew. Mine safety was not often a priority in earlier days, as men were considered dispensable. Most men worked for around 10–15 years before dying or needing to retire due to health complications from inhaling silica dust for many years. These men also did not have helmets. Hats were common until after World War I.

John J. Daly, pictured here, prospected heavily in Park City. He first mined at the Jones Bonanza Mine in Bonanza Flat but turned his attention to making claims in upper Empire Canyon just over the ridge from the Jones Bonanza. He incorporated the Daly Mining Company and opened the Daly Mine in 1881. He then incorporated the Daly West Mine in 1889. His close friend and partner in different ventures, John Judge, died in 1892. Daly bought up his friend's holdings and formed the Daly Judge Mining Company, to which he added the Anchor Mine in 1902. Daly condensed his holdings in 1920 to form the Park City Mining & Smelting Company. That company merged with the Ontario Mining Company and the Park Utah Mining Company in 1925 to form Park Utah Consolidated Mines Co.

Pictured are three miners underground at the 900-foot level of the Daly Mine. One miner holds a lighted candle in a sticking tommy, and the other two have already stuck theirs in the ore face on the wall. The middle miner holds a hand pick while the miner on right holds a larger pickaxe. The man on the left is John Judge, superintendent of the mine. He was later the contractor for the Alliance Tunnel and then an original investor in the Silver King Mining Company. While that investment would make his family rich, Judge died of silicosis, or miner's consumption, soon after its incorporation in 1892. He had a reputation for being one of the few men on the management side to spend real time in the mines, which unfortunately led to his death, like so many other miners of that time.

These are the Daly No. 1 and Daly No. 2 shafts in Empire Canyon. The group of mine buildings in the center with white smoke rising from twin plumes are the Daly No. 1, which has a large dump on the left. The second group of mine buildings along the ridgeline to the top of the photograph are the Daly No. 2. This view looks north down the canyon.

This is the Daly Mine in upper Empire Canyon. The main buildings and hoisting facility are at center. The houses to the right are probably the superintendent's home at the top of the hill and a boardinghouse beneath it. In front of the main buildings, stacks of lumber take up much of the surface outside the mine. This lumber was needed to support the structure of the mine shaft, tunnels, and rail tracks. After Park City and Snyderville were denuded, the mines had lumber shipped in from other counties and the Uintah Range of mountains to the east.

The Little Bell Mine was formed in 1880 and was a steady producer for five decades. In 1902, it was acquired by the Daly West Mine and later became part of the Park Utah Consolidated Mines Company. Pictured are the Little Bell Mine ore bins covered with snow.

Mining was difficult in the winter. Not only was it cold, but Park City gets several feet of snow each year. This horse team is struggling to make its way up to the Little Bell Mine through a tunnel dug out from a large snowdrift.

Despite what this postcard reads along the bottom, these two mines are the Quincy and the Daly West. The Quincy Mine, on the left, was incorporated in 1899 with the Putnam claim as its main holding. It quickly became one of Park City's best producers. The similarly successful Daly West Mine sat just northwest of the Quincy. Disputes about the directions of ore veins led to several lawsuits between the two mines. Ultimately, this resulted in the Daly West acquiring the Quincy in 1902 and running it as a second Daly West shaft. By folding the Quincy into its holdings, the Daly West became one of Park City's "Big Four" mines along with the Ontario, the Silver King, and the Daly Judge.

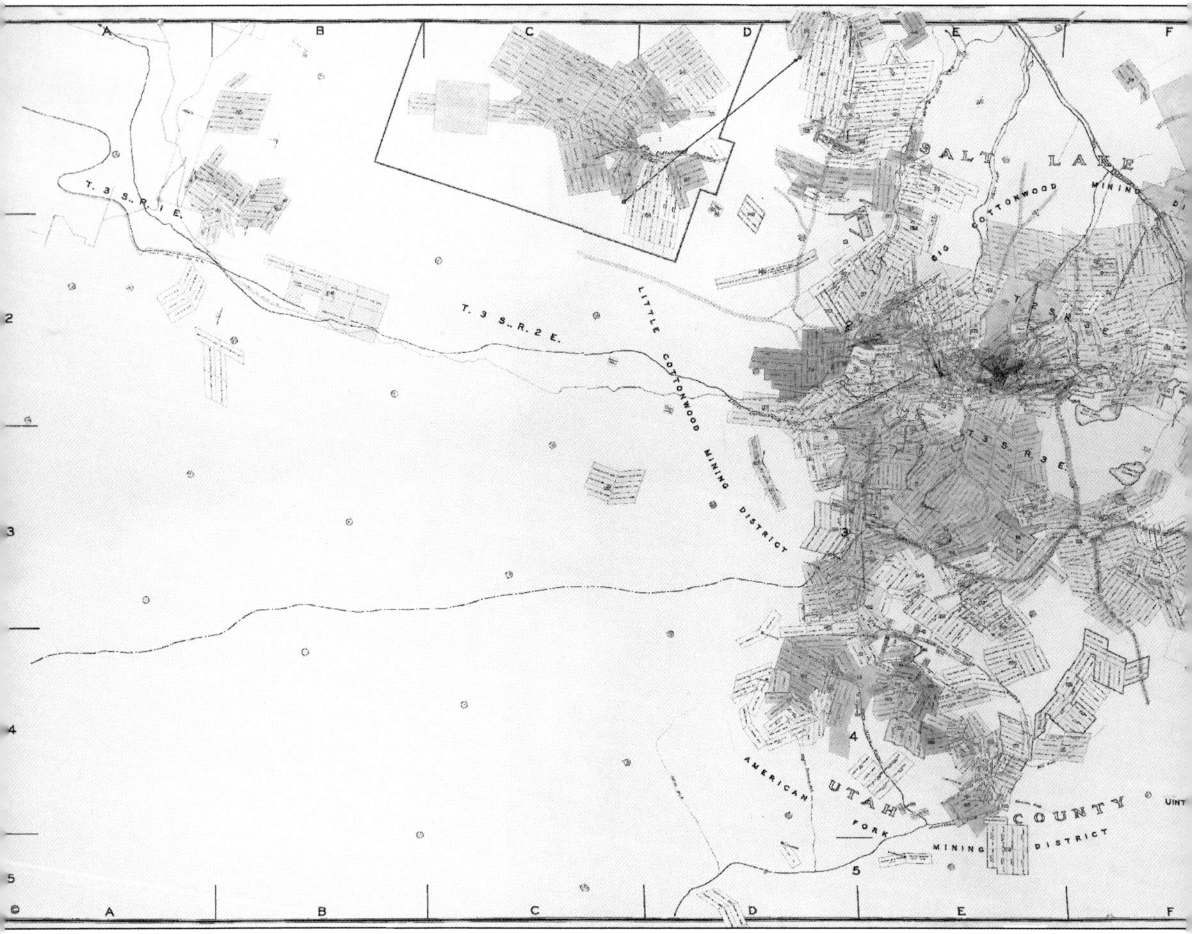

This map of mining claims shows the complexity of how claims overlapped and interacted. This map does not show, however, how those claims were made on ground that is not flat or level, but rather undulating and mountainous. It is not difficult to see how many lawsuits arose from

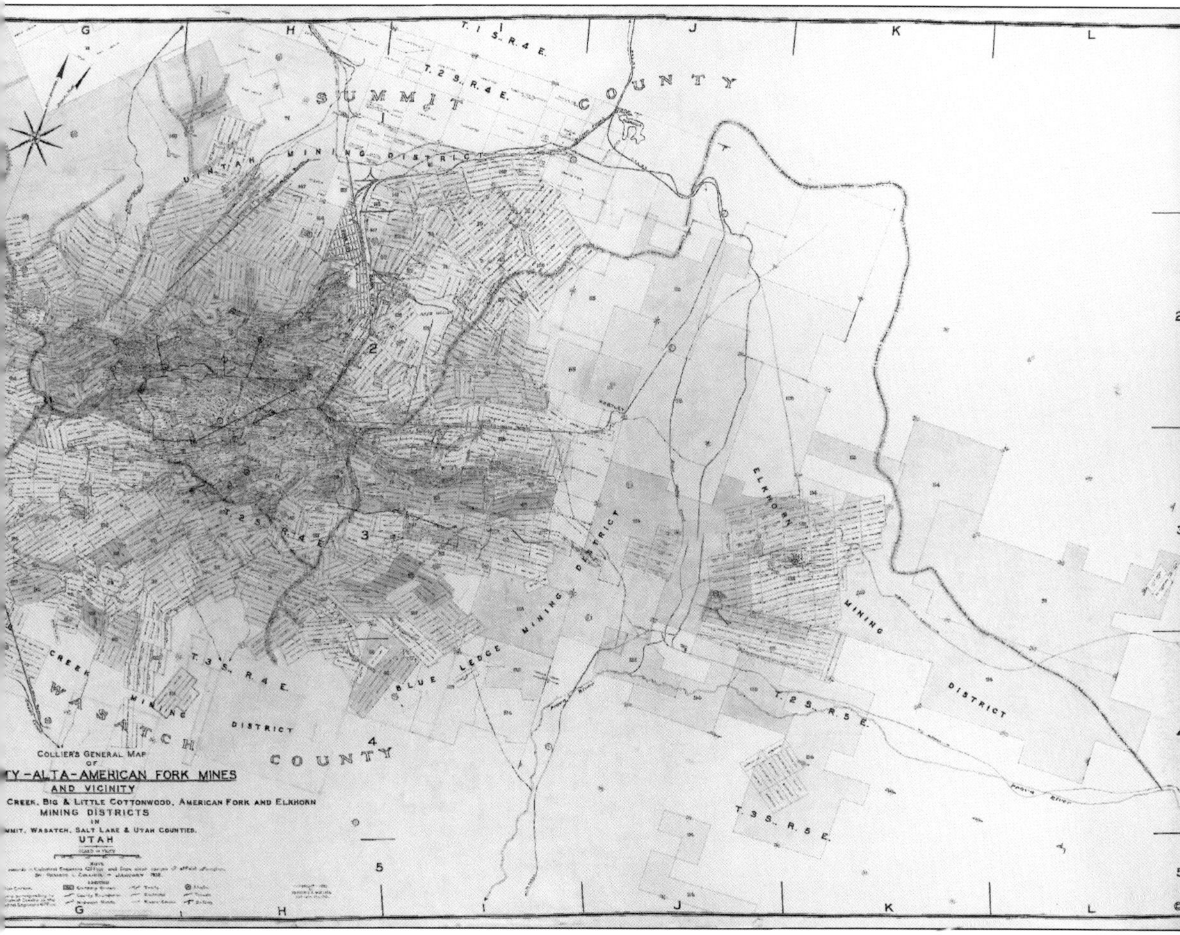

confusion surrounding whose claim had the rights to certain ore bodies. This map was updated in 1932 and includes the Park City mining area in the center. The Park City mines fell mostly in the Uintah Mining District but also the Blue Ledge and Snake Creek districts.

This photograph of the Daly Mine gives probably the clearest example of how the mines ravaged the landscape by removing all of the trees in the area for lumber. Hundreds of stumps remain on the hillside behind the mine.

Pictured is the Daly West machine shop. The man in the foreground, Klyde Peterson, is sharpening steel. To the left is Frank Archer. The men in the background, from left to right, are Wesley Young, John Birkbeck, and unidentified. Machine shops are an important part of a mine, responsible for fixing tools, making replacement pump parts or fixing broken ones, blacksmithing horseshoes, and more.

On July 15, 1902, a munitions box exploded in the Daly West Mine somewhere below the 900-foot level. Two men were killed instantly. Several men went to investigate and discovered noxious gasses at the 1,440-foot level. They ordered everyone out of the mine. Rescue efforts began shortly after, but the gasses were overwhelming, and they had also spread from the Daly West to the Ontario Mine through connected tunnels. The gasses killed another 32 men. Pictured is likely one of the funeral processions for the miners killed in the disaster. Legislation was passed in 1903 outlawing storing explosives belowground as a result of Park City's worst mining accident.

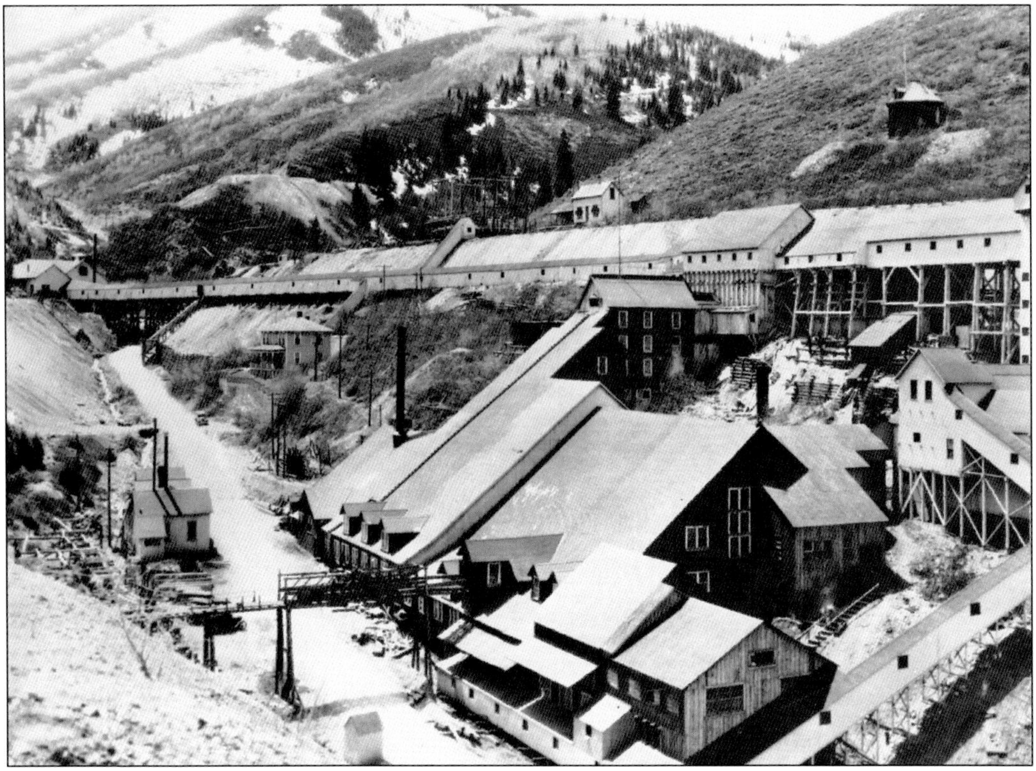

Pictured around the 1920s is the Daly Judge Mine and Mill complex in Empire Canyon at the mouth of Walker-Webster Gulch. This mine was one of Park City's most successful producers. The view is uphill to the west. A covered tramway extends from the portal of the Anchor/Judge Tunnel (left center) to the top of the mill. A large water tank is on the hillside above the mill to the upper right. The superintendent's two-story house, built in 1908, is below the tramway between the tunnel portal and the mill and has an automobile below and in front of it. John Daly incorporated this mine in 1889. It was renamed the Judge Mining & Smelting Company in 1916.

Miners stand by ore cars pulled by a mule from the Anchor Tunnel portal (the small shed behind the ore cars). Later called Judge Tunnel, it is located in Empire Canyon at the mouth of Walker Webster Gulch and served as an exit for ore cars from the Daly Judge Mine. The view is uphill to the southwest. The separate Massachusetts Mine is on the hill behind and above the tunnel portal. Waste rock from the nearby Alliance Tunnel sits on the right. Park City still mines water from this tunnel.

The Judge Mine also had an aerial tramway. The towers on the hillside are pictured here in 1963. The terminus of the tramway sat on Marsac Avenue just south of where the Marsac Mill site had been. Its abandoned remains are pictured below around the 1970s.

Pictured in this view facing southwest is the Judge Mining & Smelting Company offices and change room. Three automobiles are on the right side. The building with the smokestack partially shown to the left is the portal of the Judge Tunnel, previously called the Anchor Tunnel. This building is in Empire Canyon at the mouth of Walker-Webster Gulch above the Daly-Judge Mill site. (Courtesy of the Pop Jenks Collection, Park City Historical Society & Museum.)

The American Flag Mine was a rare gold mine among silver mines in Park City. Sitting on the east side of Empire Canyon, the mine was incorporated in 1902. Its surface buildings were destroyed in a fire in 1934, but they were quickly rebuilt. However, with declining metal prices and labor shortages from World War II, the mine closed in the 1940s. (Courtesy of the Pop Jenks Collection, Park City Historical Society & Museum.)

The Park City Consolidated Mine, called the Park Con, was the second to last entry to Park City's mining race. Opened in 1928, this mine sat away from all the others in Frog Valley, southeast of Rossie Hill, and was abundant in silver, gold, and lead. The only other mine in the area was the Queen Esther, east of Rossie Hill and north of the Park Con. The Park Con could have been one of Park City's biggest bonanzas had it been incorporated earlier. Metal prices sank just a year or so after the Park Con opened, due to the Great Depression. It scraped by because of the high value of its ore, but by the 1940s, prices had not recovered enough, and it faced a labor shortage due to World War II. The mine closed with millions of dollars of ore left untapped. The photograph above shows the Park Con Mine buildings on the edge of Frog Valley. The second image shows a miner using a jackleg drill with a hose attached. The hose sprayed water to the tip of the drill as it bore its way into the rock to prevent silica dust from filling the air. This safety improvement added years to miners' lives, as they no longer breathed in as much dust. The miner is also wearing an early hard hat, likely a "hard-boiled hat," another safety advancement.

Pictured is miners' housing in the mining community of Keetley, which was formed between 1887 and 1894 by workers constructing the Ontario Drain Tunnel No. 2 from east to west. Another group worked west to east starting from the Ontario Mine; the two groups met in the middle for the completed tunnel. Former Pony Express rider Jack Keetley headed the operation, so the tunnel and community were named for him. The Keetley miners later worked primarily in the Mayflower Mine southeast of Park City on the east side of Bald Mountain. Keetley was abandoned when Utah decided it was the best location for a reservoir to serve Wasatch County. Many of the buildings remain underwater. (Courtesy of the Pop Jenks Collection, Park City Historical Society & Museum.)

The (new) Mayflower Mine, beyond Bald Mountain to the east, was the last mine to open in Park City, but it lasted until 1972, making it the second to last to close (after the Ontario). The new Mayflower mined primarily gold, rare for Park City. It was also hot underground, also rare for Park City. Most mines were 50 to 55 degrees Fahrenheit underground. In 1961, Hecla Mining Company took over the lease and began to modernize the operation. Unfortunately, declining metal prices fell below the cost of mining and the Mayflower closed in 1972. The c. 1960s image above shows the Mayflower Mine buildings, including a mill built by Hecla. The c. 1940s image below shows the Mayflower rescue team. The men are wearing oxygen tanks and gas masks. After World War I, many mines invested in rescue and safety equipment and trained teams in rescue situations in case of emergency.

Pictured above around the 1940s are men at the bottom of the Mayflower shaft. The men are working in pairs to drill the ground beneath them and extend the shaft. The photograph was taken from above, showing the rectangular timber supports for the shaft. The gaps in the timbering would allow for a cage to go down, a manway for manual access, a slot for a bucket or dumbwaiter to send tools, and a compartment for pipes. (Not all of that is visible in the photograph.) The c. 1940s image below shows a man inspecting a vein of gold in the rock face. After an initial shaft was dug in a spot believed to contain or be near valuable ore, miners would dig tunnels at different levels and then follow veins in whatever directions they led to maximize the amount of ore that could be extracted. In other words, they did not just dig at random. The man in the photograph is also wearing a hard hat more similar to the hard hats used today.

Seven

General Life in Park City

Like any other quickly growing community, Park City needed a variety of amenities and businesses to support its population. At the very least, Park City needed a doctor, a general store or two, a grocer and butcher, a livery stable, a train depot, a schoolhouse (or several), and a lumber and coal yard. Other extras included churches, a theater, social gathering spaces, a hotel, a baker, a dentist, a laundry, a clothier, a jeweler and watchmaker, a barber, a town photographer, restaurants, and more.

Additionally, as Park City was the only non-Mormon stronghold in Utah and was full of immigrants, migrants from other states, and hard laborers, the town needed saloons. It needed many saloons not only due to the sheer number of the population who drank, but also different saloons for different ethnic groups. The Swedes had their own bar, as did the Czechs, the Irish, and most other groups. It was a way for immigrants to keep connected to others who shared their culture and customs and to dispel some of their homesickness.

Of course, life for the usually single miners in Park City would not be complete without brothels. Park City was well known to the rest of the state as a place of vice. Not only were there two dozen saloons with alcohol and gambling, but the town accepted "houses of ill repute." The row of houses where men could be "entertained" was in a designated section of town just behind the edge of Main Street. The town would fine these establishments each month for indecency, but never shut them down because of their vital role in the lives of the lonely and overworked miners.

Henry Spriggs was an important figure in Park City in 1900. He opened the Oak Saloon, with its 30-foot oak bar, on Main Street in 1902. The saloon burned in 1974; that location is now Miner's Plaza on Main. Spriggs acquired the dairy farm and ranch pictured here east of Park City and used Dority Spring Creek to create a series of ponds for fish farming. The barn still stands just east of the soccer fields at Treasure Mountain Junior High School.

About a dozen covered wagons sit in front of Lowe's Feed Stable. N.A. Jacobson, Willis Terry, John Park, and Sidney Pace sit on the two center wagons. This livery stable was at Heber and Pacific Avenues, near the Union Pacific Depot. The photograph is dated 1914 but is likely earlier. It is not impossible, however, because although Park City had plenty of automobiles by then, most miners and others would not be able to afford a car. Livery stables were an essential business for towns until cars took over. They kept horses and mules ready for whoever needed them, along with wagons and carriages.

This July 1905 photograph shows a Denver & Rio Grande engine and tender overturned as it headed north out of town to Salt Lake City. Someone had left the switch open. The open switch was not apparent to engineer Joe Bywater until it was too late to stop. He immediately threw the engines into reverse and told the fireman, George Edger, to jump. The train was scheduled to head down Parley's Canyon with three passenger cars. When Bywater threw the engines into reverse, the engine reared up in the front. When the first two cars left the track, Bywater was thrown free of the train, breaking his leg, but Edger was killed instantly when the train landed on him. Fortunately, the passenger cars stayed on the rails, sparing many lives.

Pictured are the front and rear of the June 13, 1911, Miners' Day parade. In those days, the parade was in the early summer; today, it is held on Labor Day. The route back then was to go up Park Avenue, then turn over onto Main Street, and head back downhill. The parade was a whole-town affair and provided a way for everyone to recognize the hardworking miners, whom the existence of Park City relied on.

Pictured is Susanna Bransford Emery Holmes Delitch Engalitcheff, Utah's Silver Queen. Her first marriage was to Albion Emery in 1884. She and Albion invested in the Silver King Mining Company with a loan from R.C. Chambers, which made them rich. Albion died young, and Susanna moved to Salt Lake, where she began life as a socialite, hosting parties and traveling the world. Most of her subsequent husbands died within several years of marrying her. Notably, R.C. Chambers sued her for half her shares in the Silver King Mining Company only three months after Albion died (he had not left a completed will), but she won the lawsuit. A more complete account of this suit, involving many of Park City's most prominent people, can be found in Judy Dykman and Colleen Whitley's book *The Silver Queen*.

Park City attracted workers from all over the country and the world. As such, a variety of Christian denominations formed churches in town. All of the pictured churches, except St. Mary's, were built in Park City after the Great Fire of 1898. From left to right are the Latter-Day Saints Ward, the Congregational Church (later known as the Community Church), St. Mary's Catholic Church, St. Luke's Episcopal Church, and the Methodist church.

After the Union Pacific Railroad was completed about 30 miles north of Park City, the burgeoning mining town needed a connecting spur to that major line. Many of the Chinese rail workers who had helped complete the railroad also built the spur from Echo down to Park City. Many decided to stay in Park City after completing the spur. Not welcomed among the white neighborhoods sprouting up to the west of Main Street or on Rossie Hill, they built a small Chinatown on the lower half of Swede Alley. By 1893, Chinese Americans made up about 10 percent of Park City's population. Pictured is a Chinese cook in a boardinghouse.

Chinese Parkites were heavily discriminated against. The Michigan Bunch who ran the Marsac Mill and lived on Rossie Hill funded the construction of a bridge in 1888, pictured above from a distance, that allowed those who lived on Rossie Hill to bypass Chinatown and walk straight to Main Street at Fourth Street. The bridge was badly damaged in the fire of 1898 but was rebuilt afterward. The great fire destroyed most of Chinatown. Most whites refused to help the Chinese rebuild, so many Chinese left Park City. Those who stayed endured enough discrimination that by the 1920s, only three families remained. The bridge was replaced by a smaller walkway and stairs in 1915, which stood until 1954. That version is pictured in the head-on view at right.

Born in 1851 in Missouri, Jane Parker had moved to Park City with her son by 1887. Though seldom seen on the streets, she became a respected member of the Park City community. Parker catered special events, making delicacies like the pictured five-tiered wedding cake. The *Park Record* reported that "great prestige was bestowed upon a hostess who could employ the services of this much sought-after woman."

Every town needed a general store, and Park City needed several. Perhaps the most prominent, Welsh, Driscoll, & Buck is pictured here sometime after rebuilding from the great fire. The left side of the business sold clothing, boots and shoes, and furniture, among other things, while the right side sold dry goods and perishables.

An entire family of nine sits on a sled on one of Park City's western streets, likely Woodside Avenue. Children spent a lot of time playing in the snow growing up in Park City. There was little else to do. One favorite pastime was sledding down Woodside Avenue, which was usually not plowed in the winter. Sledders would start at the peak of upper Woodside around Third Street and sled all the way to the high school nine blocks away.

Pictured is a bandstand on the old site of the Marsac Mill on July 4, 1918. The *Park Record* called it the "Best Fourth of July Celebration in Park City Ever." It estimated 40,000 people viewed that year's parade, after which several thousand gathered to listen to a patriotic speech by a visiting Catholic clergyman and then watch "the Grand Pageant of Nations" at the bandstand. The pageant depicted freedom emerging from oppression through song and Lady Liberty parading through flags of various countries. This took place as World War I raged in Europe.

Social activity is a large part of any community. To keep children occupied, Parkites hosted classes and other activities. Pictured is Ms. Langford's dance class in 1919. This photograph was taken by Pop Jenks, one of the town's early photographers who also ran a soda fountain and a restaurant.

It was hard for people in town to escape anything to do with the mines. Smoke hovered in the valley from trains shipping ore and mills processing it. Mining structures also sat in all sections of town. The Silver King Coalition Building sits prominently in the center of this 1912 view of Park City looking west, while the Silver King aerial tramway extends from the Coalition Building up Treasure Hill in the background. The Denver & Rio Grande train station and warehouse extends to the right. The view reaches from Seventh Street on the left to Ninth Street on the right.

Miners needed ways to blow off steam after working such difficult and dangerous jobs. Several of the mines sponsored baseball teams for their workers. Baseball was quite popular in Park City, and mines and fraternal organizations fielded teams that squared off against one another. Pictured here is a squad from the Ontario Mine around the 1910s. The young boy in the middle was likely the batboy.

In 1936, Park City consolidated the three presidentially named elementary schools (Washington, Jefferson, and Lincoln) into the new Marsac School, pictured here, which is city hall today. Park City's population had not only leveled off, but many families had to leave town in search of other jobs after the Great Depression affected the mines. The new school was built by the Works Progress Administration as part of the New Deal. It originally served grades one through eight while the high school served grades nine through twelve. Kindergarten joined the Marsac School in 1947. (Courtesy of the Pop Jenks Collection, Park City Historical Society & Museum.)

Park City High School opened a few weeks into the 1927–1928 school year, providing Park City with a larger, more modern facility for its children. A mechanical arts building was added in 1936 as part of another Works Progress Administration project. The high school, pictured behind the football field, served grades nine through twelve from 1927 through 1976, when a new high school was built. The 1927 school now houses the Park City Library. The school offered core classes, as well as many extracurriculars, including the yearbook, theater, band, many clubs, and many sports. The football team is in action in the 1946 image above. The image below shows students in geometry class in 1947.

Carrie Vivian Hodgson arrived in Park City in 1904 and ran a jeweler's shop at 363 Main Street until her death in 1968. The store, pictured above, sold jewelry, watches, clocks, cameras, and lamps, among other things, and was well-known on the Wasatch back. Hodgson was also the official Union Pacific timekeeper for many years, the Park City weatherperson (until her eyesight failed her near the end of her life), and an avid horse rider. She had a lot of personality, on display in the portrait of her at left. Almost everyone in town knew her and loved her—everyone except her husband, anyway. In defiance of societal expectations of women in the 1910s, Carrie divorced her husband, Charles, kept the store, and began a life of legendary romance with some of Park City's bachelors while maintaining a highly regarded reputation in her business and social circles. According to the divorce file, she had regularly "sought the society of men" (and, reportedly, women) who were not her husband—both in their home and elsewhere. Charles, after learning of her infidelity, confronted Carrie, who told him the matter was "none of his business."

Generally considered Park City's first skier, Emmett "Bud" Wright utilized skis to access the town's telephone poles in the winter, which stretched from town to the operational mines all over the hills. Wright is pictured here holding his mismatched skis at the Keystone Mine in the early 1920s. He broke the tip off one of his skis at some point, but continued to use the two different lengths.

Just below the Creole Mine, Parkites set up a ski jump in the 1930s—the first recreational skiing in town that would eventually become one of the great ski destinations in the world. The jump was not especially large but attracted locals and others from Utah. This jump would be superseded by the world-renowned Ecker Hill jump out near Kimball Junction. Here, an unidentified man soars off the jump.

Parkites loved to celebrate holidays, and a local favorite has always been Halloween. Different organizations held dances and balls with costume contests, apple bobbing, decorations, and other festivities. Many people also threw parties for their friends. Children played many pranks, like soaping windows and tipping outhouses. Pictured here are students celebrating at the Marsac School.

After King Tut's tomb was uncovered in 1922, a craze of Egyptian-style architecture and décor flashed through the United States. Park City was no exception, and built the Egyptian Theater in 1926. Pictured here in 1949, the theater was the premier spot for theater productions and traveling shows, but screened films as well. For a time in the 1960s and 1970s, the theater façade was replaced, but it was restored in the 1980s with the advent of the Sundance Film Festival.

On February 19, 1942, Pres. Franklin D. Roosevelt signed Executive Order 9066, authorizing the incarceration of people of Japanese ancestry, including American citizens. The US government forcibly moved 120,000 people of all ages from the west coast to 10 relocation camps. The order allowed for an incredibly slim amount of time when the Japanese and Japanese Americans were able to relocate themselves if they could. Fred Wada was able to broker a four-year lease for 3,500 acres that included an apartment house with a man who owned most of the land around Keetley, just outside of Park City. He and his family, along with 14 other families, moved their lives there and opened a farm (pictured) for the duration of World War II. From left to right are Frank Rivers, Fred Wada, and possibly Charlie Tusumoto. (Courtesy of the Utah State Historical Society.)

As cars became the go-to mode of transportation, several garages opened in Park City. This one, Eley Motors, pictured in 1949, was at the corner of Heber and Park Avenues. The Silver King Aerial Tramway is visible behind the garage.

City hall is pictured around the 1920s–1930s. The mayor and other government employees took the top floor, the fire department took up the tower and back room, and the territorial jail served Park City until roughly 1966. The sheriff's office was across the street. The city moved to the Marsac School building in 1983. The historical society opened a museum here in 1984, which persists to this day.

Attached to the city hall building was the Park City Library. The pictured one-room library served as Park City's library from 1921 until 1982, when it was moved to the newly relocated Miners Hospital building at City Park. To move the books, Parkites formed a line—called the Book Brigade—that stretched three quarters of a mile from the old location to the new and passed books hand to hand over the course of one day. The Book Brigade is pictured below on September 4, 1982, passing the Union Pacific railyard.

Eight

Depression and Reevaluation of Economy

Between July 1952 and 1953, Park City lost nearly one third of its population. Lead-zinc and silver prices had fallen drastically and were stagnant at depressed prices. The Silver King Mining Coalition and Park Utah Consolidated Mines both ceased operations as the cost of mining ore was greater than what could be made from it. Nearly 800 miners were laid off. *Business Week* magazine wrote of Park City, "parts of the once-thriving town already look like a ghost village. Houses stand empty with their windows smashed. Half the stores in town are boarded up. Many have been closed for some time, but at least eight have gone out of business since last December. The population . . . is now down to about 1,500."

The *Park Record* called the town "an island of depression in Utah's prosperous, expanding economy." Miners were hoping that mining companies could lobby Congress to improve the prices of precious metals, but there was little prospect of that. Instead, United Park City Mines, now the owner of most Park City mines, had to think outside of the mine tunnels—to the mountain surface.

Park City was run down in the 1950s. Not by choice, of course. The economy was booming elsewhere, but metal prices did not improve much, and most of the mines remained closed or limited. Without money flowing into town, upkeep slumped. Some businesses were abandoned. But even those that were fully operational, like city hall and the library pictured here in June 1955, looked like no one was home.

From the 1950s through the 1970s, Park City lost many buildings from its mining era. Some people moved and took their homes with them. Other buildings were left to waste away. This building at 338 Main Street was lost to the latter fate.

Many of the mine structures began to fall apart as well. Shafts especially need constant upkeep. Otherwise, they deteriorate and collapse, taking the surface hoist structures with them. A few of the mines remained open, struggling to break even, but most were left behind, like the small mine pictured here on part of the future site of Park City's next venture: skiing. To try and recoup money from losses they were suffering in mining, United Park City Mines Company leased its surface rights on Treasure Hill for the new Treasure Mountains ski resort to open in 1963.

United Park City Mines had taken over all of Park City's mines except the new Mayflower in 1953 and continued extracting ore from a few—mostly the Ontario. In 1970, the largest shareholders created Park City Ventures to operate the Ontario. They held on for a few years, but economic turbulence in the 1970s dashed most of their hopes to keep mining alive in Park City. Pictured is the Ontario No. 3 shaft and related buildings in 1974, under the management of Park City Ventures.

United Park City Mines had already leased its surface rights on Treasure Hill for the Treasure Mountains ski resort (called Park City Ski Area by 1975). In 1975, it began looking to lease the rest of its surface rights in Ontario Canyon, Empire Canyon, and Deer Valley. It found a partner in the Royal Street Corporation and its CEO, Edgar Stern, to build Deer Valley Resort. In a last-ditch effort to keep the Ontario Mine running, Park City Ventures leased that operation to Canadian mining conglomerate Noranda in 1979. It could not scrape by and had to close shop in 1982, just as Deer Valley was wrapping up its first successful ski season. Pictured is a tattered Noranda banner asking for mine workers, a fitting representation of Park City's last gasp at mining the silver that put it on the map. The reins were now fully turned over to the ski industry—a story for another time.

INDEX

aerial tramway, 53, 63, 68, 69, 73, 97
American Flag Mine, 98
Bonanza Flat, 7, 22, 87
California Comstock Mine/Mill, 53, 74, 75
Chambers, R.C., 79, 83, 84, 107
Chinatown, 7, 41, 108, 109
city hall, 45, 47, 48, 121, 122, 124
Cornish Pump, 85, 86
Creole Mine, 64, 118
Crescent Mine, 56
Daly, John, 87, 96
Daly Judge Mine, 22, 79, 81, 87, 96
Daly Mine, 87–89, 94
Daly West Mine, 8, 22, 79, 87, 91, 94, 95
Flagstaff Mine, 7, 17–19, 22, 81
Friends of Ski Mountain Mining History, 6, 75
Hodgson, Carrie Vivian, 116
Judge, John, 87, 88
Judge Mine/Mill, 97, 98
Kearns, Thomas, 23, 57, 60, 62
Keetley, 79, 85, 100
Keith, David, 23, 57, 60, 62
Lake Flat, 17, 20-22
Little Bell Mine, 79, 90
Mayflower Mine (original), 23, 24, 53, 57, 60, 62
Mayflower Mine (new), 23, 79, 100–102, 125
Miners Hospital, 38, 39
Northland Mine, 57, 61, 62
Ontario Mine, 7, 20–22, 79, 81-87, 100, 125, 126
Park City Consolidated Mine (Park Con), 79, 99
Park Utah Consolidated Mining Company, 79, 87
Quincy Mine, 22, 79, 91
railroads, 7, 10, 11, 32, 33, 35, 53, 56, 69, 73, 103–105, 108, 113
schools, 8, 29, 36, 103, 114, 115
Silver King Coalition building, 53, 68, 69
Silver King Coalition Mines Company, 53, 76–79
Silver King Consolidated Mine (King Con), 53, 64, 70–75
Silver King Mine/Mill, 23, 53, 57–59, 61–70
Silver King Mining Company, 7, 23, 53, 56–57, 59–62, 64, 78, 88
Silver Queen, 60, 107
Snyderville, 7, 9, 10, 12, 14–16, 24
Spiro, Solon, 70, 74, 76
Spiro Tunnel, 76, 77
Treasure Hill, 7, 25, 53–56, 64, 78, 125, 126
United Park City Mines Company, 53, 79, 123, 125, 126
Woodside Mine, 25, 53, 57

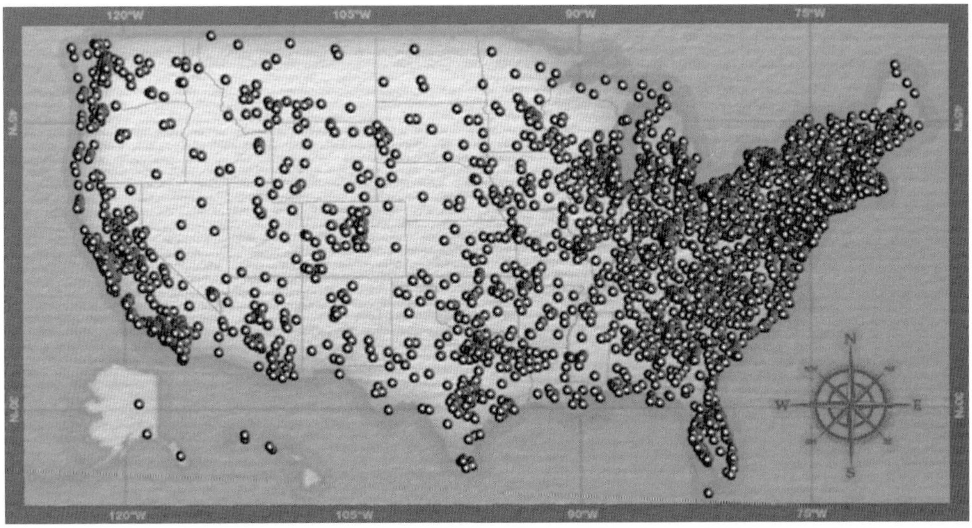

Consistent with our mission to preserve history on a local level, this book was printed in South Carolina on American-made paper and manufactured entirely in the United States. Products carrying the accredited Forest Stewardship Council (FSC) label are printed on 100 percent FSC-certified paper.

MADE IN THE USA